My First Note-Reading Book
Mein erstes Notenlesebuch

by Kerstin Wartberg

Supplement 1 with CD · Ergänzungsband 1 mit CD

Mike Hoover
Translation from the German Text

Gino Romero Ramirez
Djembé (African drum) · Djembé (Afrikanische Trommel)

David Andruss
Piano *and* Piano arrangements for all recorded pieces
Klavier und Klavierarrangements für alle aufgenommenen Stücke

Ingo Klatt
Sound Engineer · Aufnahmeleitung

Recorded in the Steinway-Haus Heinersdorff, Düsseldorf, Germany
Aufgenommen im Steinway-Haus Heinersdorff, Düsseldorf

© 2006 Summy-Birchard Music
division of Summy-Birchard Inc.

ISBN 0-7390-4232-7

Exclusive print rights administered by Alfred Publishing Co., Inc.
All rights reserved

Foreword

Geleitwort

Dr. Shinichi Suzuki,
Waltraud Suzuki,
Kerstin Wartberg

How wondrous is the life force! One feels it everywhere. Through it we can enjoy the beauty of nature. Tiny buds become magical flowers, every morning the birds begin to sing, and countless leaves, grasses, and flowers herald to us the great life force. In addition to the magnificence of nature, we have also been given the gift of music. Music is the language of the spirit and should purify us and open our hearts for the sublime. We need to recognize that this gift is to be used. Sixty years ago, when I recognized the scope and mighty power of nature's developmental principles and realized that every child in the world learns his mother tongue without difficulty, I changed the outlook on my life and made countless discoveries. We should all learn to be an integral part of creation and not to oppose the life force. Once this is learned, we can reach unbelievable heights. Our task as parents and teachers is to raise our children to be worthy people who will be able to assume responsibility for the further development of the world. Much is to be done. With courage, enterprise, and gratitude for the life force that is given to us, we can travel this road together.

Kerstin Wartberg was the first German to study at and graduate from the Talent Education Institute in Matsumoto, Japan. In the many years since then, my wife and I have been in close contact with her.

I am pleased that she wants to share my teaching method and philosophy with the interested reader. I wish her publication a large circulation and hope that it falls on fertile ground.

Wie wundervoll wirkt die Lebenskraft! Überall ist sie zu spüren. Sie ermöglicht, daß wir uns an der Schönheit der Natur erfreuen können. Wir beobachten, wie die Knospen sich zu zauberhaften Blüten öffnen, wie jeden Morgen die Vögel wieder zu singen beginnen und wie unzählige Blätter, Gräser und Blumen uns von der großen Lebenskraft künden wollen. Zu der herrlichen Natur ist uns außerdem noch die Musik geschenkt worden. Musik ist die Sprache des Geistes und soll uns läutern und für Höheres öffnen. Wir Menschen müssen erkennen, daß wir diese Geschenke nutzen sollen. Als ich vor etwa 60 Jahren den Umfang und die gewaltige Kraft der natürlichen Entwicklungsgesetze erkannte und feststellte, wie jedes Kind auf der Welt seine Muttersprache problemlos erlernt, habe ich mein Leben umgestellt und danach unzählige Entdeckungen gemacht. Wir alle sollten lernen, uns nicht gegen die Lebenskraft zu stellen, sondern uns in die Schöpfung einzufügen. Dann werden wir, von den großen Hilfen gestärkt, unglaubliche Höhen erreichen können. Die Aufgabe der Eltern und Lehrer ist, unsere Kinder zu wertvollen Menschen zu erziehen, die später einmal die Verantwortung für die Weiterentwicklung der Welt übernehmen können. Vieles ist zu tun. Mit Mut, Tatkraft und Dankbarkeit für die uns geschenkte Lebenskraft können wir den Weg gemeinsam gehen.

Kerstin Wartberg war die erste Deutsche, die am Talent Education Institute in Matsumoto/Japan studierte und graduierte. Sie steht seitdem nun schon über viele Jahre mit meiner Frau und mir in enger Verbindung.

Ich freue mich, daß sie meine Unterrichtsweise aus methodisch-didaktischer und aus übergeordneter Sicht dem interessierten Leser nahebringen will. So wünsche ich ihren Veröffentlichungen eine weite Verbreitung und hoffe, daß sie auf fruchtbaren Boden fallen werden.

Matsumoto, June/Juni 1994

Shinichi Suzuki

Introduction

"My First Note-Reading Book" with its companion CD can be used parallel to the lesson books "Step by Step" or with any other violin method. It leads young violinists, step by step and in a playful manner, through the basics of reading music and sight reading. Learning goals include:

1. Command of basic rhythms
2. Learning all tones on all strings in the first finger-pattern

The book is divided into four parts:

1. Speech, clapping and motion games

In the first part of the book, elementary note values are introduced. All rhythms can be heard on the CD, played by drum and piano, and encourage the children to take up the pulse in a lively manner. Rhythms introduced here form the foundation for all following chapters.

2. Drawing games, writing games, brain teasers

Appearing between the short, easily understood exercises are numerous drawing games, writing games and brain teasers. Not only entertaining, these are also an interesting way to introduce note-reading and note-writing. Solutions to the brain teasers can be found on the last two pages.

To give this book a personal touch, students may want to color the drawings.

3. Note-reading exercises with and without the instrument

All notes in the first finger-pattern will be introduced and systematically practiced in this book. Accidentals are always included where required, but their meaning will not be explained until the next book.

As students work through the exercises, the following practice variations are recommended to ensure that the notes in each five-tone group are thoroughly mastered:

    a) Careful study of the short note sequence
    b) Singing with a rhythm text
    c) Singing with finger numbers
    d) Singing with note names
    e) Playing with pizzicato
    f) Playing with the bow
    g) Playing with the CD

The piano arrangements on the CD are purposefully kept simple so that students will not be distracted from learning the pitches. Every short exercise has an introduction of two measures which musically introduces the new concept to be learned.

4. Training in sight-reading

After thoroughly working through the material, the student should gradually increase the number of tunes played with the CD in sequence until all forty-eight tunes can be played without interruption.

And now I should like to wish all my young music making friends, their parents, and their teachers, joy and success in working through the note-reading book!

Kerstin Wartberg

Einleitung

Das erste Notenlesebuch mit zugehöriger CD kann neben den Übungsheften *Schritt für Schritt*, aber auch neben jeder anderen Violinschule verwendet werden. Hier wird der junge Geigenschüler auf spielerische Weise Schritt für Schritt in die Grundlagen des Notenlesens und Blattspielens eingeführt. Lernziele dieses Heftes sind u.a.:

1. Beherrschung elementarer Rhythmen
2. Systematische Erarbeitung aller Töne auf allen Saiten in der ersten Griffstellung

Das vorliegende Buch ist in vier Lernabschnitte aufgeteilt:

1. Sprech-, Klatsch- und Bewegungsspiele

Im ersten Teil des Buches werden elementare Notenwerte vorgestellt. Alle Rhythmen sind mit Trommel und Klavier auf der zugehörigen CD eingespielt und regen die Kinder an, den Puls durch Sprech-, Klatsch- und Bewegungsspiele ganz lebendig in sich aufzunehmen. Die hier vorgestellten Rhythmen bilden die Grundlage für die weiteren Kapitel.

2. Mal- und Schreibspiele, Notenrätsel

Zwischen kurzen, leicht verständlichen Übungen sind zahlreiche Mal- und Schreibspiele sowie Notenrätsel zu finden, die zum einen sehr unterhaltsam sind und zum anderen den Kinder einen interessanten Einstieg in das Notenlesen und -schreiben geben. Die Auflösungen der Rätsel sind auf den letzten beiden Seiten abgedruckt.

Damit das Notenlesebuch eine ganz persönliche Note bekommt, können alle Bilder ausgemalt werden.

3. Notenleseübungen mit und ohne Instrument

In diesem Heft werden alle Noten in der ersten Griffstellung erlernt und systematisch geübt. Die Vorzeichen sind zwar bei allen kurzen Liedchen aufgeführt. Ihre Bedeutung wird aber erst im nächsten Heft erklärt.

In der Erarbeitungsphase werden folgende Lernschritte für die Lieder im Fünftonraum empfohlen:

    a) Genaues Anschauen des kurzen Notentextes
    b) Singen mit dem Rhythmustext
    c) Singen mit der Fingerzahl
    d) Singen mit den Notennamen
    e) Zupfen
    f) Greifen und streichen
    g) Spielen mit der Begleit-CD

Die Klavierarrangements auf der Begleit-CD sind bewußt einfach gehalten, um die Konzentration uneingeschränkt auf das Erlernen der Tonhöhen zu lenken. Jede kleine Übung hat ein Vorspiel von zwei Takten, in dem schon der neue Lernschritt musikalisch angekündigt wird.

4. Blattspieltraining

Nach einer gründlichen Erarbeitungsphase sollen immer mehr Liedchen hintereinander mit CD-Begleitung gespielt werden, bis das Kind am Ende alle 48 Stücke im Block spielen kann.

Nun bleibt mir nur noch, meinen kleinen musizierenden Freunden, ihren Eltern und Lehrern viel Freude und Erfolg beim Arbeiten mit dem Notenlesebuch zu wünschen!

Kerstin Wartberg

Contents · Inhalt

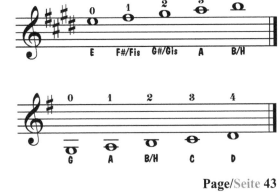

Benny walks

Benny wandert

Listen to the CD selection with the walking-notes several times and perform the following actions:

♦ Walk like Benny through the room. The drum indicates how fast you should walk, each drum beat representing one step.

♦ Now clap and walk to the drum beat. As you do, speak the following rhythm text clearly:

Ben - ny's walk - ing. Ta ta ta ta.
Ben - ny's walk - ing. Ta ta ta ta.

♦ On the facing page, point to each note in turn while speaking the rhythm text clearly.

Höre Dir das Liedchen mit den Wandernoten mehrmals auf der CD an und führe dazu folgende Bewegungen aus:

♦ Wandere wie Benny durch das Zimmer. Die Trommel gibt Dir Dein Schritttempo an. Jeder Trommelschlag ist ein Schritt.

♦ Klatsche und gehe nun mit dem Trommelschlag. Sprich dazu laut und deutlich den Rhythmustext:

Ben - ny wan - dert. Ta ta ta ta.
Ben - ny wan - dert. Ta ta ta ta.

♦ Zeige mit dem Zeigefinger auf die nebenstehenden Noten und sprich dazu laut und deutlich den Rhythmustext.

A walking note (quarter or crotchet note) looks like this!

It has a black head and a stem that can be drawn either up or down.

So sieht die Wandernote (Viertel Note) aus!

Sie hat einen schwarz ausgemalten Notenkopf und einen Notenhals, der nach oben oder nach unten zeigen kann.

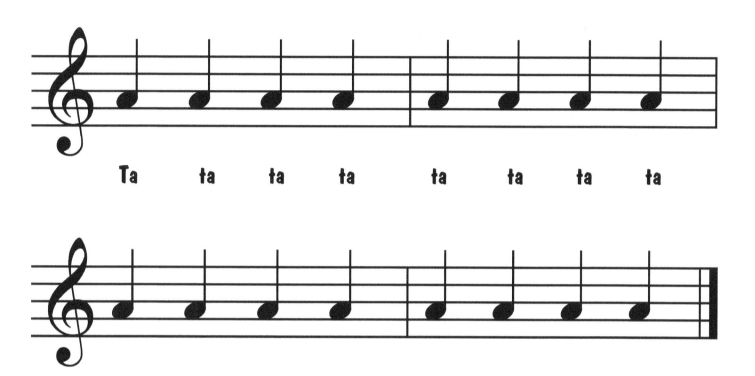

Ta   ta   ta   ta   ta   ta   ta   ta

Copy our first tune on the staff below!

Schreibe unser erstes Liedchen noch einmal ab!

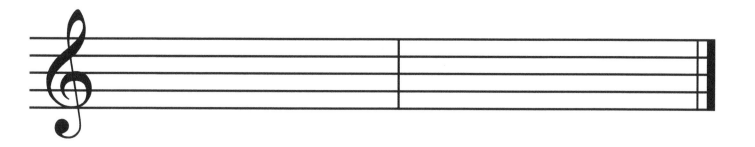

Benny hops — Benny springt

Can you hop like Benny around the room? After each hop take a brief rest.

Kannst Du auch wie Benny durch das ganze Zimmer hüpfen? Lege nach jedem Sprung eine kurze Pause ein.

♦ Speak the following text exactly in rhythm:

   Hop – sh – Hop – sh ...
   or
   Ta – sh – ta – sh ...

♦ Sprich dazu deutlich den Rhythmustext:

   Sprung – scht – Sprung – scht ...
   oder
   Ta – scht – ta – scht ...

♦ Clap your hands energetically during **Ta** and place your index finger in front of your mouth during the rest (**sh**).

♦ Klatsche bei **Ta** kräftig in die Hände und führe während der Pause (bei **scht**) Deinen Zeigefinger vor Deinen Mund.

♦ On the facing page, point to each note in turn while speaking the rhythm text clearly.

♦ Zeige mit dem Zeigefinger auf die nebenstehenden Noten und sprich dazu laut und deutlich den Rhythmustext.

The walking note (quarter or crotchet note) and the walking rest (quarter or crotchet rest) look like this!

So sieht die Wandernote (Viertel Note) und so die Wanderpause (Viertel Pause) aus!

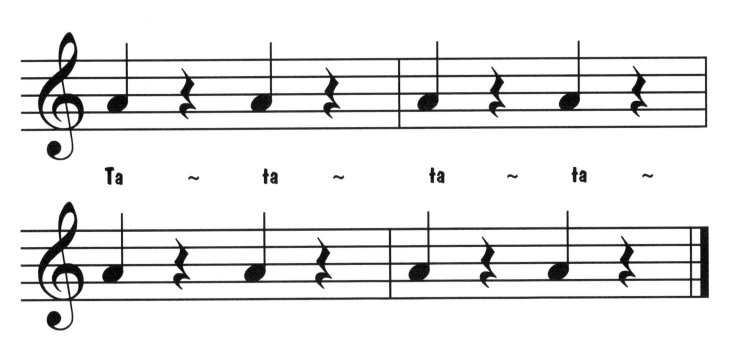

Ta ~ ta ~ ta ~ ta ~

Copy our second tune on the staff below!

Schreibe unser zweites Liedchen noch einmal ab!

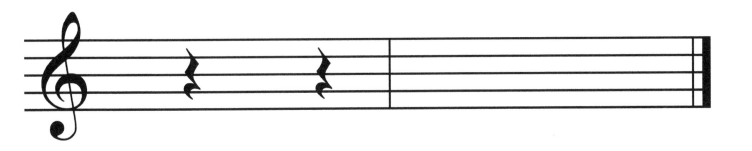

Benny strolls

Benny bummelt

Listen to the CD selection with the strolling notes and...

Höre Dir das Liedchen mit den Bummelnoten auf der CD an und ...

♦ ... stroll slowly through the room like Benny. The drum gives you the tempo. Every drum beat represents one step. Say the rhythm text as you stroll:

Ta-o ta-o ta-o...

♦ Can you take a big step during **Ta** and bend your knees slightly during **-o**? These movements will help you feel if all strolling notes are equally long.

♦ ... clap together with the drum during Ta and drop both hands during **-o.**

♦ On the facing page, point to each note in turn while speaking the rhythm text clearly.

♦ ... gehe ganz langsam wie Benny durch das Zimmer. Die Trommel gibt Dir das Tempo an. Jeder Trommelschlag ist ein Schritt. Sprich dazu laut und deutlich den Rhythmustext: **Ta-o ta-o ta-o...**
Kannst Du auf **Ta** einen großen Schritt machen und auf **-o** einen kleinen Knicks? Durch die beiden Bewegungen fühlst Du leicht, ob alle Bummelnoten gleich lang sind.

♦ ... klatsche gemeinsam mit der Trommel auf **Ta** und lasse auf **-o** beide Hände nach unten fallen.

♦ ... zeige mit dem Zeigefinger auf die Noten und sprich dazu laut und deutlich den Rhythmustext.

A strolling note (half or minim note) looks like this!

It's note head is **not** filled in. It also has a stem that can point up or down.

The strolling note is held for two beats and is twice as long as the walking note (quarter or crotchet note).

So sieht die Bummelnote (Halbe Note) aus!

Ihr Notenkopf ist **nicht** ausgemalt. Sie hat einen Notenhals, der nach oben oder nach unten zeigen kann.

Die Bummelnote wird zwei Schläge ausgehalten und ist doppelt so lang wie die Wandernote (Viertel Note).

Ta – o   ta – o   ta – o

Copy our third tune on the staff below!

Schreibe unser drittes Liedchen noch einmal ab!

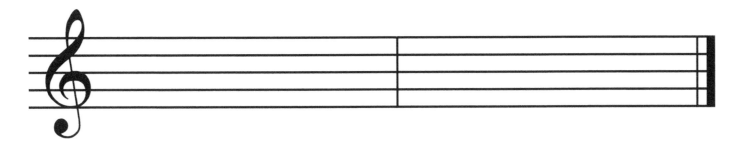

Benny sleeps

Benny schläft

Listen to the CD selection with the sleeping notes and...

♦ ... speak the rhythm text clearly:

Ta – o – a – o.

♦ ... clap together with the drum on **Ta** and move your arms during the other syllables outward and inward.

♦ ... follow the notes on the facing page with your index finger while speaking the rhythm text.

Höre Dir das Schlafnotenliedchen auf der CD an und ...

♦ ... sprich dazu laut und deutlich den Rhythmustext: **Ta – o – a – o.**

♦ ... klatsche gemeinsam mit der Trommel auf **Ta** in die Hände und bewege bei den anderen Silben die Arme rhythmisch nach außen und innen.

♦ ... zeige mit dem Zeigefinger auf die nebenstehenden Noten und sprich dazu laut und deutlich den Rhythmustext.

A sleeping note (whole or semibreve note) looks like this!

Its note head is **not** filled in and it does **not** have a stem.

The sleeping note is held for four beats.

It is twice as long as a strolling note (half or minim note) and four times as long as the walking note (quarter or crotchet note).

So sieht die Schlafnote (Ganze Note) aus!

Ihr Notenkopf ist **nicht** ausgemalt und sie hat **keinen** Notenhals.

Die Schlafnote wird vier Schläge ausgehalten.

Sie ist doppelt so lang wie die Bummelnote (Halbe Note) und viermal so lang wie die Wandernote (Viertel Note).

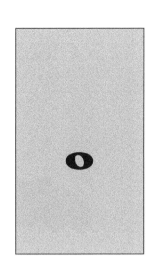

Ta - o - a - o   ta - o - a - o

Copy our fourth tune on the staff below!

Schreibe unser viertes Liedchen noch einmal ab!

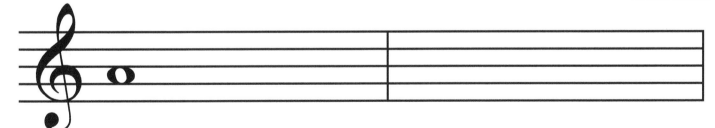

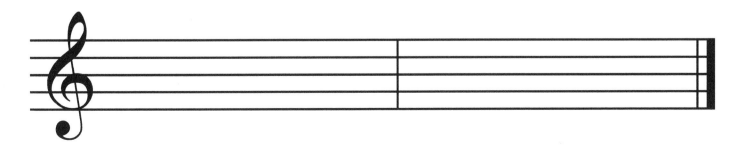

13

Children run

Kinder laufen

Running notes (eighth or quaver notes) look like this!

Two running notes (eighth notes or quaver notes) are as long as one walking note (quarter or crotchet note).

They can be written several different ways:

So sehen Laufnoten (Achtel Noten) aus!

Zwei Laufnoten (Achtel Noten) sind gemeinsam so lang wie eine Wandernote (Viertel Note).

Sie können auf verschiedene Arten aufgeschrieben werden:

a) **Singly** / Einzeln

b) **In pairs** / Zu zweit

c) **Four together** / Zu viert

All the kids are running quickly

Alle Kinder laufen schneller

Clap the running notes while speaking a rhythm text:

All the kids are running quickly
'cause it's getting really windy
or Titi titi titi titi   titi titi titi titi.

Klatsche die Laufnoten und sprich dazu den Rhythmustext:

Alle Kinder laufen schneller,
denn der Himmel wird nicht heller
oder Titi titi titi titi   titi titi titi titi.

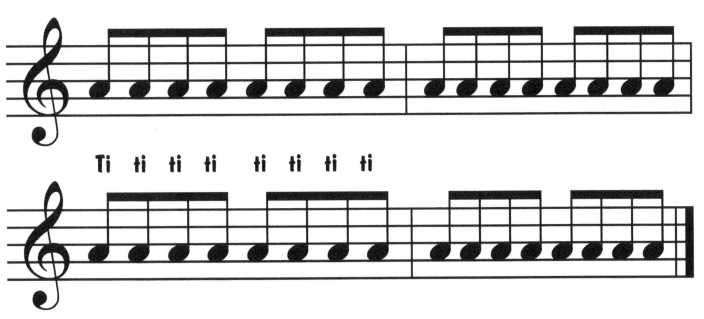

 ## Running quickly home now

Laufen schnell nach Hause

Clap this exercise with running and strolling notes while speaking a rhythm text:

All the kids are running quickly home now or
All the dogs are running quickly home now or
All the birds are flying quickly home now or
Titi titi titi titi   ta-o ta-o.

Klatsche das Liedchen mit den Lauf- und den Bummelnoten und sprich dazu den Rhythmustext:

Alle Kinder laufen schnell nach Hau - se oder
Alle Hunde laufen schnell nach Hau - se oder
Alle Vögel fliegen schnell nach Hau - se oder
Titi titi titi titi   ta-o ta-o.

Drawing Game * Malspiel

Which clef is correct? • **Welcher ist der richtige Notenschlüssel?**

Outline the correct clef with your index finger. Always follow the arrows.
After that try to write several clefs with a pencil.

Fahre mit dem Zeigefinger auf der Linie des richtigen Notenschlüssels entlang. Folge immer den Pfeilen.
Probiere danach, mit einem Bleistift einige Notenschlüssel zu schreiben.

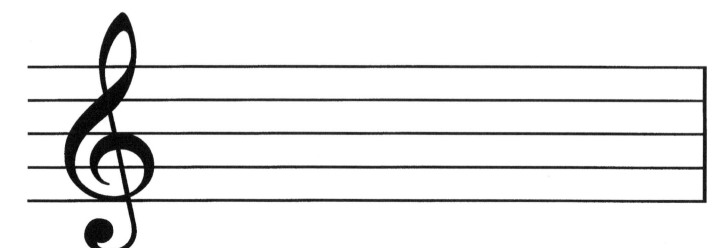

The Staff

A staff consists of five lines with four spaces.

Notes can be drawn either **on the lines**

Das Notensystem

Ein Notensystem besteht aus fünf Linien und vier Zwischenräumen. Die Noten können entweder **auf die Linien** geschrieben werden

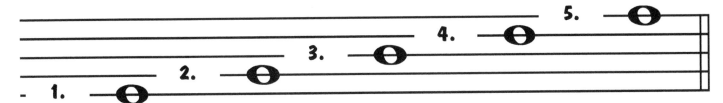

or **in the spaces**.

oder **in die Zwischenräume.**

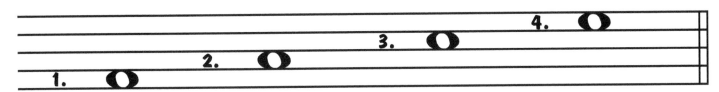

Color notes **red** that are **on lines.** Notes **in the spaces** should be colored **green**.

Male alle Noten, die **auf den Linien** stehen, **rot** aus und alle Noten, die **in den Zwischenräumen** notiert sind, **grün**.

What determines the direction of the note stem?

For notes **below the middle line,** the stem should go **up** from the **right** side of the note-head, as shown in the upper colored staff.

For notes **on or above the middle line,** the stem should extend **down** from the **left** side of the note-head, as shown in the lower staff.

Wann zeigt der Notenhals nach oben und wann nach unten?

Bei allen Noten, die **unter der dritten Linie** stehen, zeigt der Hals nach **oben**, so wie in der ersten buntausgemalten Notenzeile.
Bei allen Noten, die **auf oder über der dritten Linie** stehen, zeigt der Hals nach **unten**, so wie in der zweiten buntausgemalten Notenzeile.

Fun with Note Circles

Copy this page onto sturdy cardboard, then cut along all of the solid black lines. Arrange the pieces into new note circles. Have fun!

Das Notenscheibenspiel

Kopiere diese Seite auf eine stabile Pappe, und schneide die Notenscheiben aus. Setze die einzelnen Teile zu neuen Notenscheiben zusammen. Viel Spaß dabei!

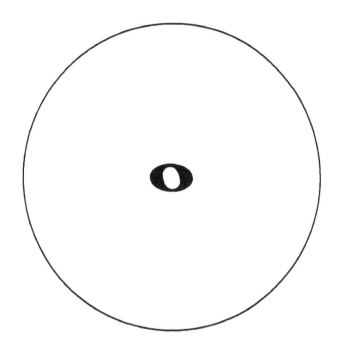

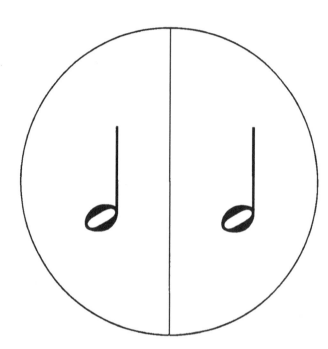

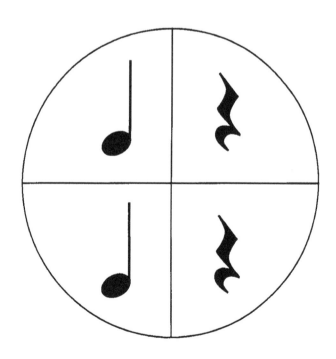

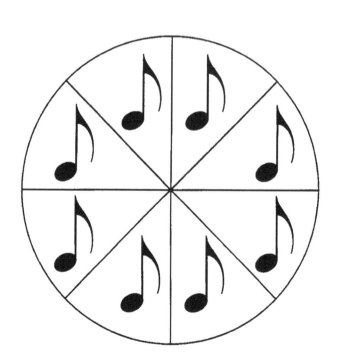

Now that you have rearranged the pieces into new note circles, write the results in the staves below. Each circle represents one measure.

Hast Du es geschafft, die Notenscheiben neu zusammen zu setzen? Dann kannst Du die Ergebnisse in die Notenlinien schreiben. Jede Scheibe erhält einen Takt.

First Game - Erstes Spiel

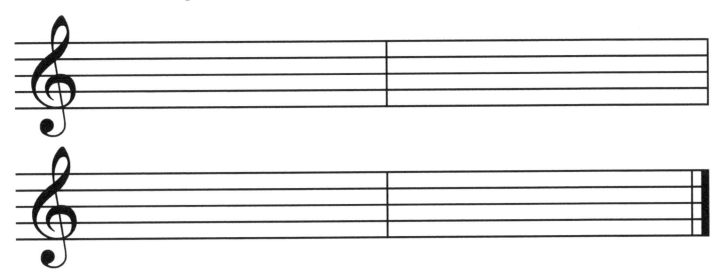

Second Game - Zweites Spiel

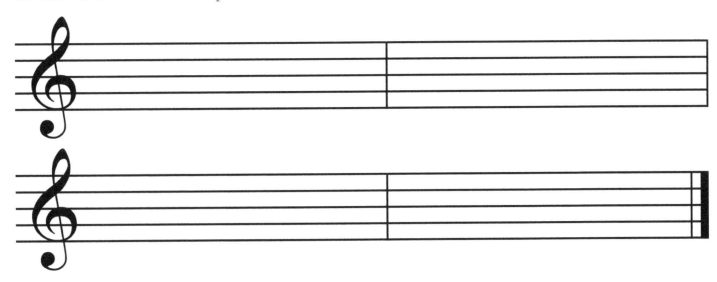

Third Game - Drittes Spiel

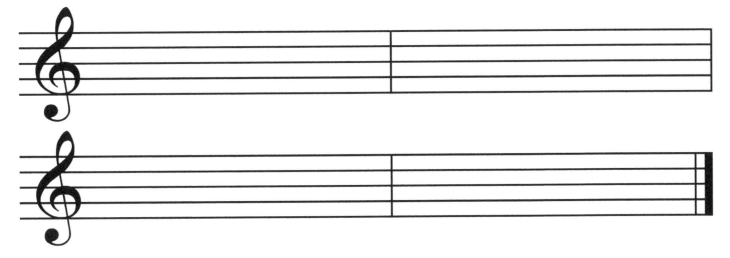

Little Tunes on the **D** String – Lieder auf der **D**-Saite

Piano Introduction for the Tunes 8 and 9 - Klaviervorspiel für die Liedchen 8 und 9

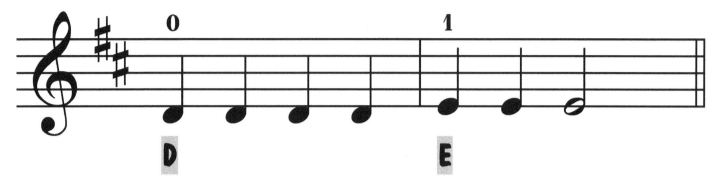

First Tune on the D String with D and E
Erstes D-Saiten-Liedchen mit den Tönen D und E

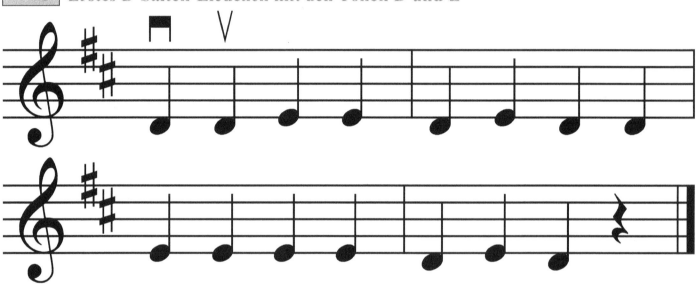

Second Tune on the D String with D and E
Zweites D-Saiten-Liedchen mit den Tönen D und E

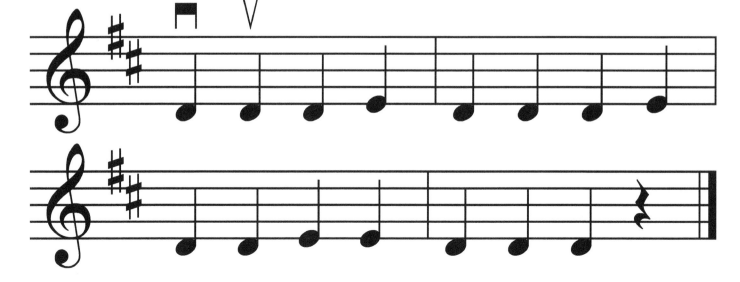

Piano Introduction for the Tunes 10 and 11 - Klaviervorspiel für die Liedchen 10 und 11

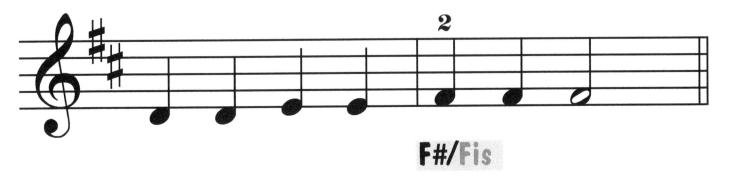

F#/Fis

First Tune on the D String with D, E and F-Sharp
Erstes D-Saiten-Liedchen mit den Tönen D, E und Fis

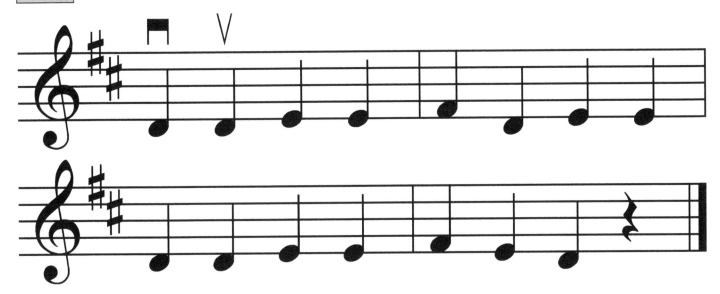

Second Tune on the D String with D, E and F-Sharp
Zweites D-Saiten-Liedchen mit den Tönen D, E und Fis

Piano Introduction for the Tunes 12 and 13 - Klaviervorspiel für die Liedchen 12 und 13

First Tune on the D String with D, E, F-Sharp and G
Erstes D-Saiten-Liedchen mit den Tönen D, E, Fis und G

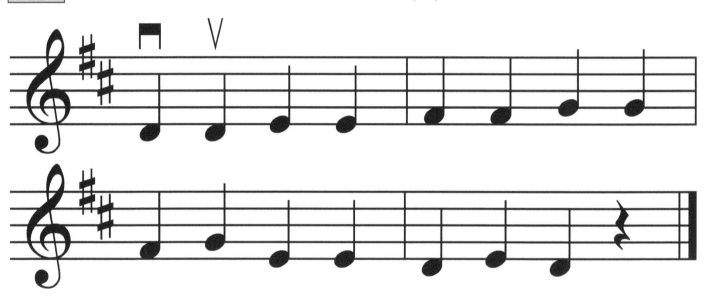

Second Tune on the D String with D, E, F-Sharp and G
Zweites D-Saiten-Liedchen mit den Tönen D, E, Fis und G

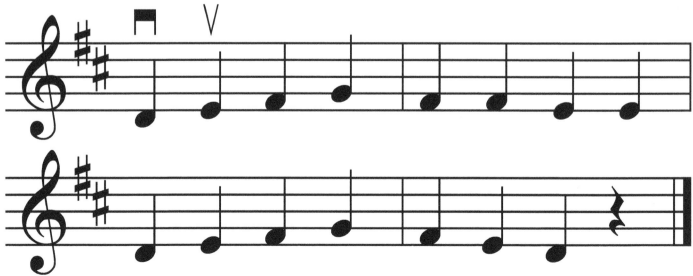

Piano Introduction for the Tunes 14 and 15 - Klaviervorspiel für die Liedchen 14 und 15

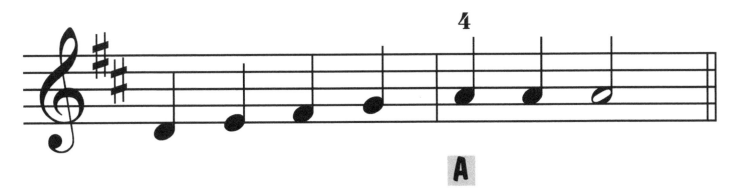

First Tune on the D String with D, E, F-Sharp, G and A
Erstes D-Saiten-Liedchen mit den Tönen D, E, Fis, G und A

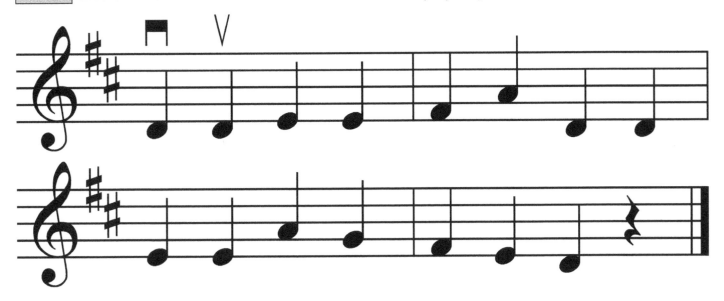

Second Tune on the D String with D, E, F-Sharp, G and A
Zweites D-Saiten-Liedchen mit den Tönen D, E, Fis, G und A

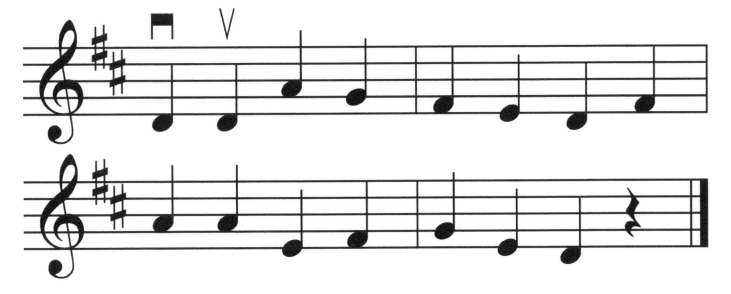

16 Benny Hops on the D String · Benny springt auf der D-Saite

17 Benny Strolls on the D String · Benny bummelt auf der D-Saite

18 Benny Sleeps on the D String · Benny schläft auf der D-Saite

19 Benny Runs on the D String · Benny läuft auf der D-Saite

24

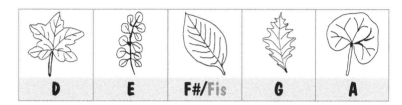

D	E	F#/Fis	G	A

As shown above, each leaf represents a different note. Your task is to write the missing note names below each leaf and then to draw each note on the staff below.

When you have finished, you will find a short melody that appears in this book.
This page looks especially beautiful if you color each leaf a different color.

Jedes Blatt gehört zu einer Note. Deine Aufgabe ist es, die fehlenden Notennamen unter die Blätter zu schreiben und die dazugehörige Note in die Notenlinien zu malen.
So entsteht ein kleines Liedchen, das in diesem Heft aufgeschrieben ist.
Diese Rätselseite sieht besonders schön aus, wenn Du jedes Blatt mit einer anderen Farbe ausmalst.

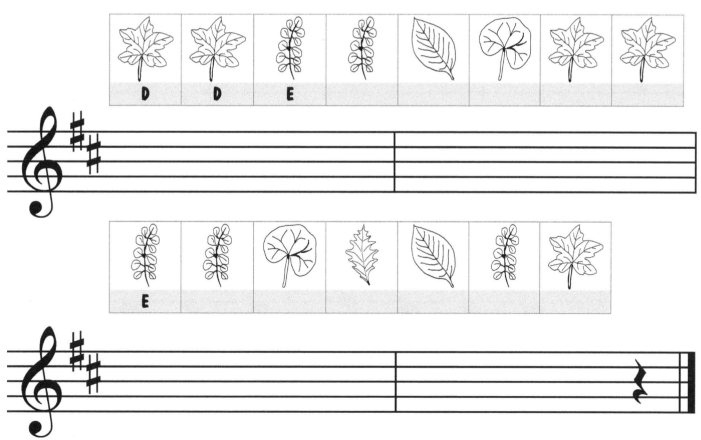

Which number is this "Leaf Melody" in the book?
Welche Nummer hat das Blätter-Lied in diesem Heft?

Little Tunes on the **A** String – Lieder auf der **A**-Saite

Piano Introduction for the Tunes 20 and 21 - Klaviervorspiel für die Liedchen 20 und 21

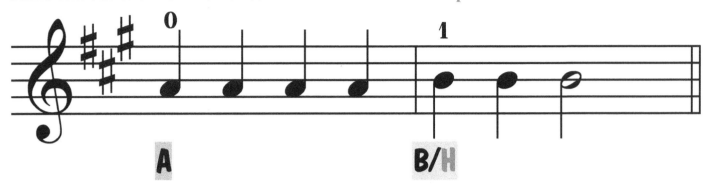

First Tune on the A String with A and B
Erstes A-Saiten-Liedchen mit den Tönen A und H

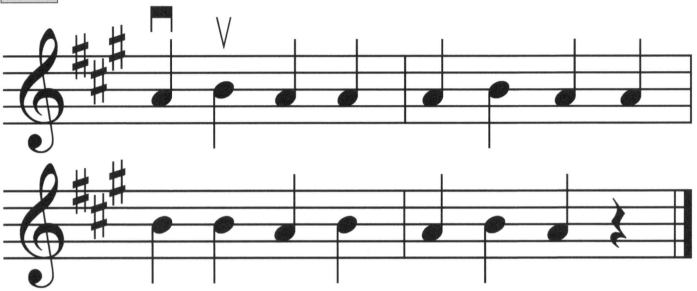

Second Tune on the A String with A and B
Zweites A-Saiten-Liedchen mit den Tönen A und H

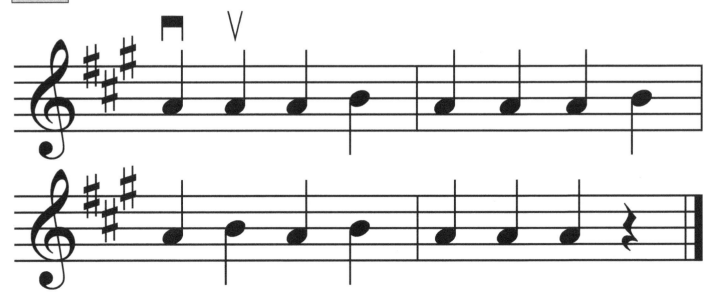

Piano Introduction for the Tunes 22 and 23 - Klaviervorspiel für die Liedchen 22 und 23

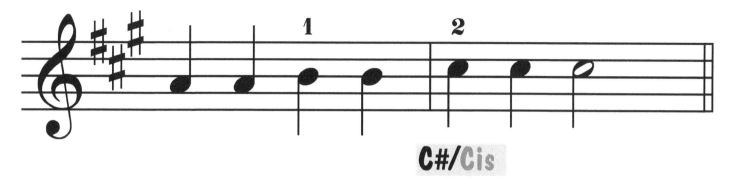

C#/Cis

First Tune on the A String with A, B and C-Sharp
Erstes A-Saiten-Liedchen mit den Tönen A, H und Cis

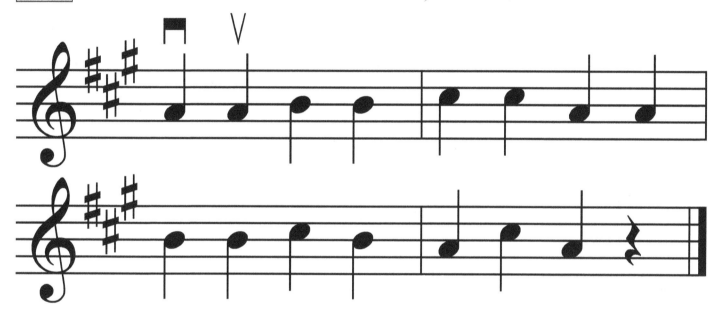

Second Tune on the D String with A, B and C-Sharp
Zweites A-Saiten-Liedchen mit den Tönen A, H und Cis

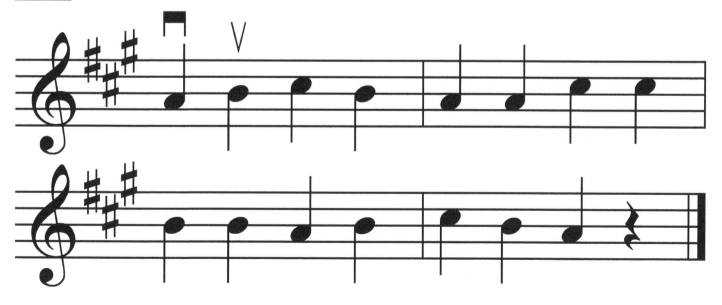

Piano Introduction for the Tunes 24 and 25 - Klaviervorspiel für die Liedchen 24 und 25

First Tune on the A String with A, B, C-Sharp and D
Erstes A-Saiten-Liedchen mit den Tönen A, H, Cis und D

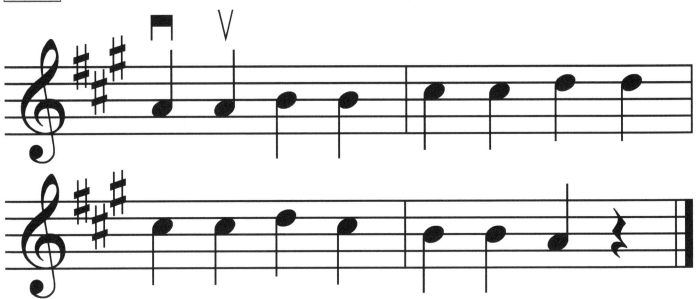

Second Tune on the A String with A, B, C-Sharp and D
Zweites A-Saiten-Liedchen mit den Tönen A, H, Cis und D

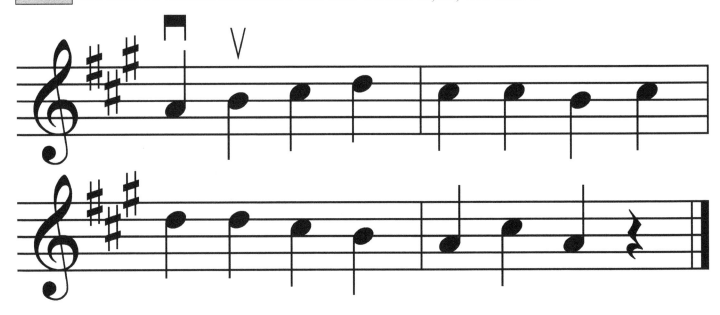

Piano Introduction for the Tunes 26 and 27 - Klaviervorspiel für die Liedchen 26 und 27

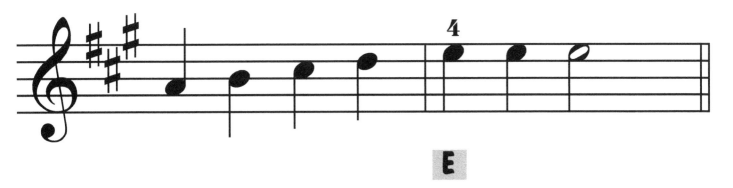

 26 **First Tune on the A String with A, B, C-Sharp, D and E**
Erstes A-Saiten-Liedchen mit den Tönen A, H, Cis, D und E

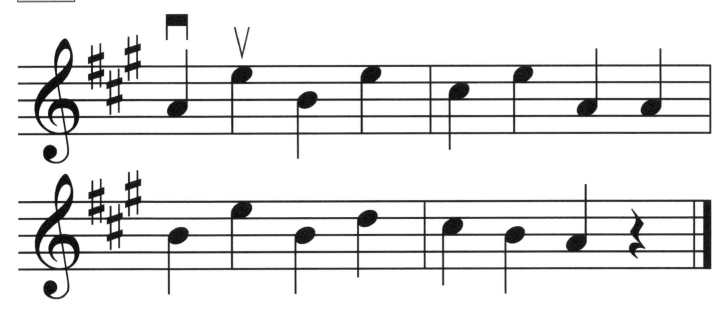

 27 **Second Tune on the A String with A, B, C-Sharp, D and E**
Zweites A-Saiten-Liedchen mit den Tönen A, H, Cis, D und E

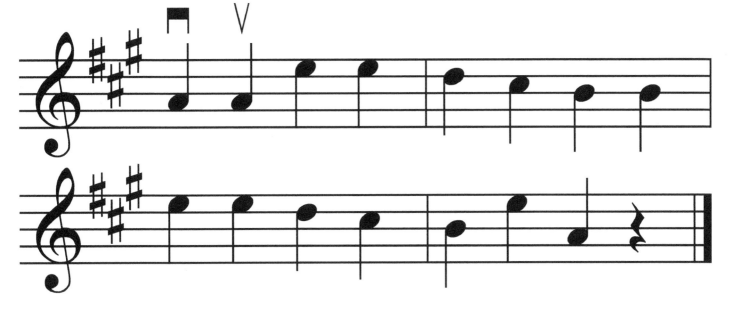

28 Benny Hops on the A String • Benny springt auf der A-Saite

29 Benny Strolls on the A String • Benny bummelt auf der A-Saite

30 Benny Sleeps on the A String • Benny schläft auf der A-Saite

31 Benny Runs on the A String • Benny läuft auf der A-Saite

It's raining notes!

Es regnet Noten!

Enter the note names in the boxes below the notes and draw the notes from the raindrops above in their proper places on the staff. This is the beginning of a familiar song, but which?

Schreibe Notennamen in die Kästchen unter den Noten und male die Noten aus den Regentropfen an die richtige Stelle in die Notenlinien. Zusammen ergibt sich daraus der Anfang eines bekannten Liedchens - nur welches?

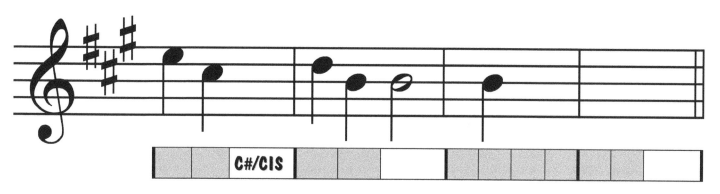

		C#/CIS									

Name of this song:
Das Lied heißt:

Little Tunes on the E String – Lieder auf der E-Saite

Piano Introduction for the Tunes 32 and 33 - Klaviervorspiel für die Liedchen 32 und 33

First Tune on the E String with E and F-Sharp
Erstes E-Saiten-Liedchen mit den Tönen E und Fis

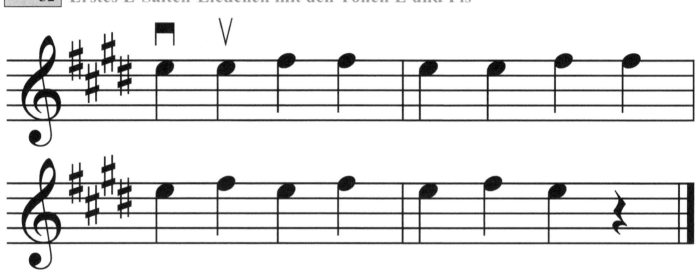

Second Tune on the E String with E and F-Sharp
Zweites E-Saiten-Liedchen mit den Tönen E und Fis

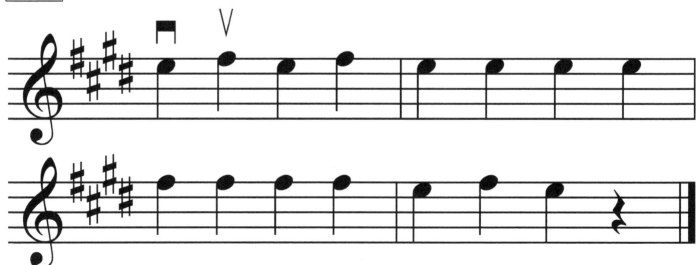

Piano Introduction for the Tunes 34 and 35 - Klaviervorspiel für die Liedchen 34 und 35

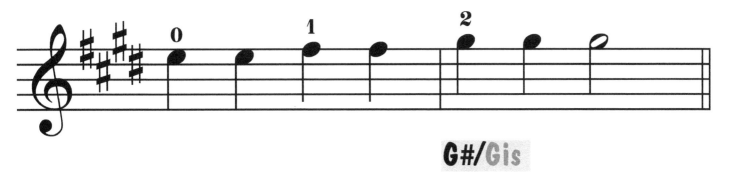

G#/Gis

 34 **First Tune on the E String with E, F-Sharp and G-Sharp**
Erstes E-Saiten-Liedchen mit den Tönen E, Fis und Gis

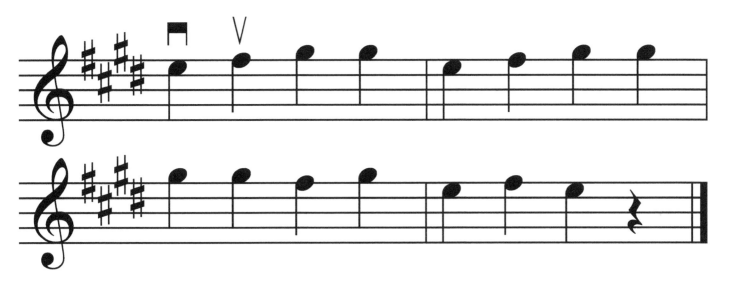

 35 **Second Tune on the E String with E, F-Sharp and G-Sharp**
Zweites A-Saiten-Liedchen mit den Tönen E, Fis und Gis

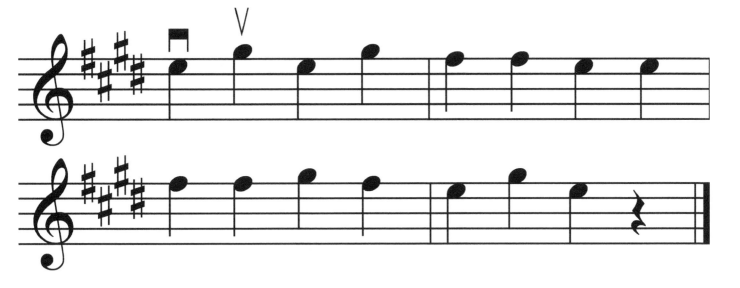

Piano Introduction for the Tunes 36 and 37 - Klaviervorspiel für die Liedchen 36 und 37

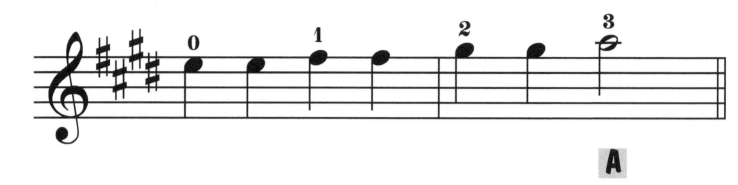

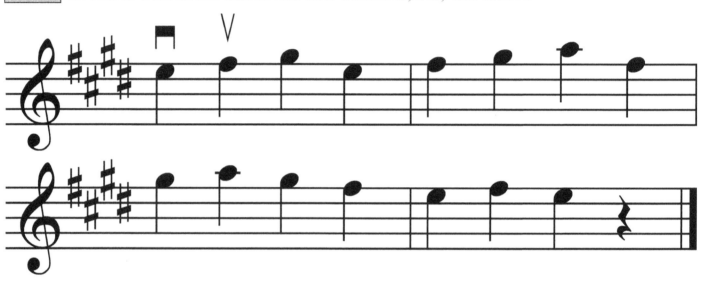

First Tune on the E String with E, F-Sharp, G-Sharp and A
Erstes E-Saiten-Liedchen mit den Tönen E, Fis, Gis und A

Second Tune on the E String with E, F-Sharp, G-Sharp and A
Zweites E-Saiten-Liedchen mit den Tönen E, Fis, Gis und A

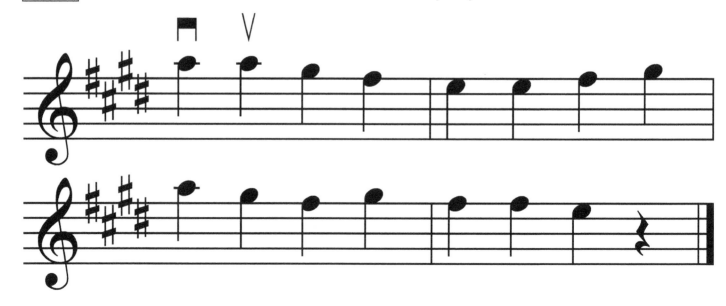

Piano Introduction for the Tunes 38 and 39 - Klaviervorspiel für die Liedchen 38 und 39

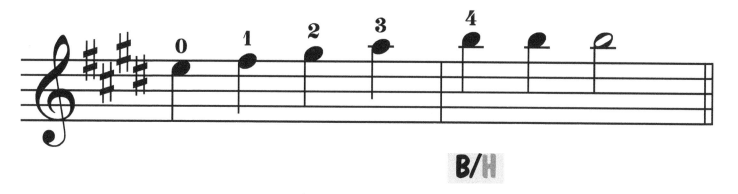

B/H

38
First Tune on the E String with E, F-Sharp, G-Sharp, A and B
Erstes E-Saiten-Liedchen mit den Tönen E, Fis, Gis, A und H

39
Second Tune on the E String with E, F-Sharp, G-Sharp, A and B
Zweites E-Saiten-Liedchen mit den Tönen E, Fis, Gis, A und H

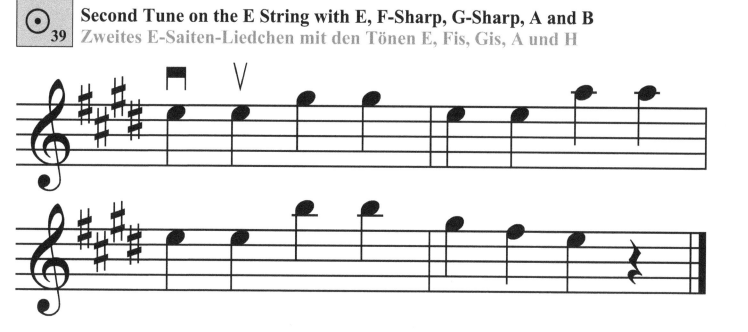

40 Benny Hops on the E String · Benny springt auf der E-Saite

41 Benny Strolls on the E String · Benny bummelt auf der E-Saite

42 Benny Sleeps on the E String · Benny schläft auf der E-Saite

43 Benny Runs on the E String · Benny läuft auf der E-Saite

36

Brain Teaser No. 3 * Ratespiel Nr. 3

Find the ten mistakes in the lower version and circle them!

Finde die 10 Fehler im unteren Lied und kreise sie ein!

Tune on the E string

Lied auf der E-Saite

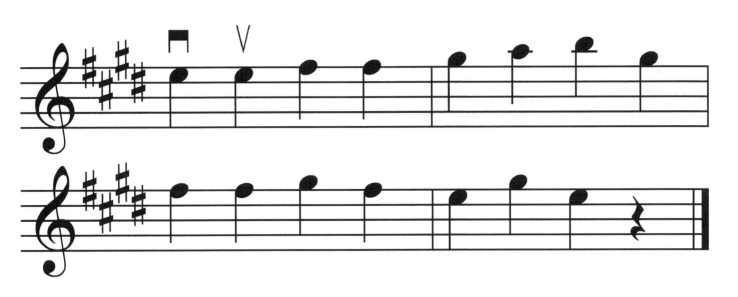

Tune on the E string with 10 mistakes

Lied auf der E-Saite mit 10 Fehlern

Little Tunes on the G String – Lieder auf der G-Saite

Piano Introduction for the Tunes 44 and 45 - Klaviervorspiel für die Liedchen 44 und 45

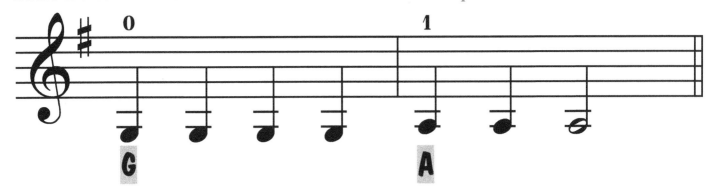

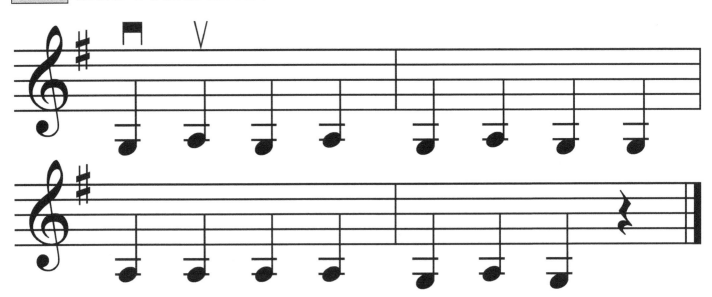

44 First Tune on the G String with G and A
Erstes G-Saiten-Liedchen mit den Tönen G und A

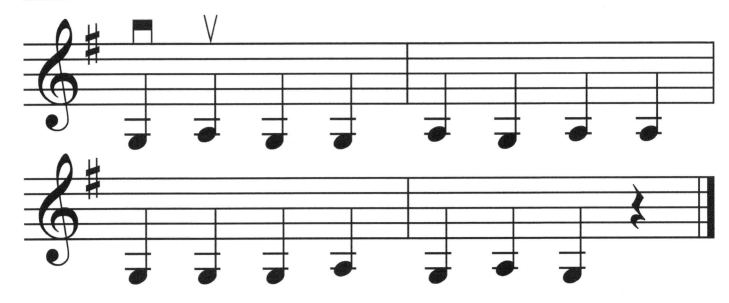

45 Second Tune on the G String with G and A
Zweites G-Saiten-Liedchen mit den Tönen G und A

Piano Introduction for the Tunes 46 and 47 - Klaviervorspiel für die Liedchen 46 und 47

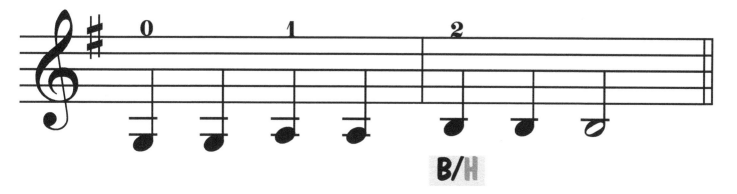

46 **First Tune on the G String with G, A and B**
Erstes G-Saiten-Liedchen mit den Tönen G, A und H

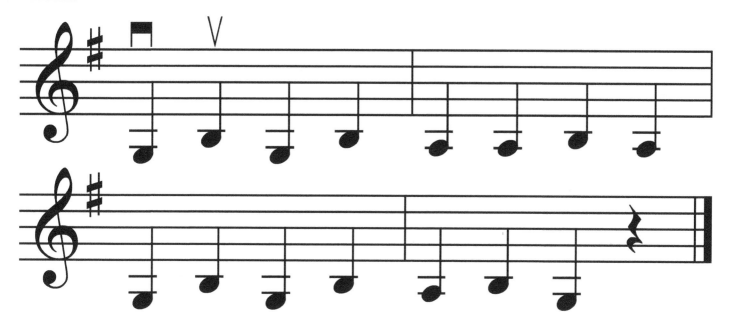

47 **Second Tune on the G String with G, A and B**
Zweites G-Saiten-Liedchen mit den Tönen G, A und H

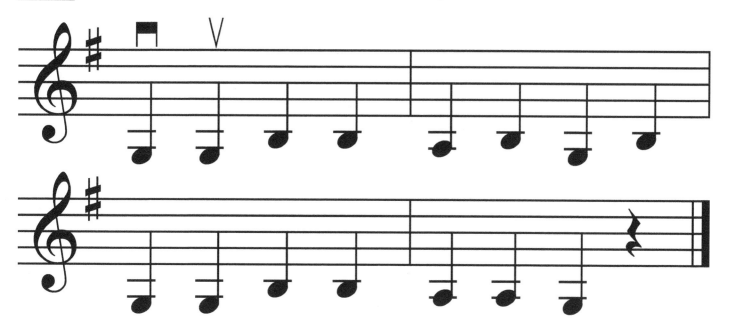

Piano Introduction for the Tunes 48 and 49 - Klaviervorspiel für die Liedchen 48 und 49

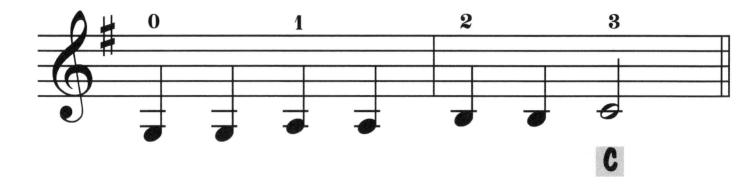

First Tune on the G String with G, A, B and C
Erstes G-Saiten-Liedchen mit den Tönen G, A, H und C

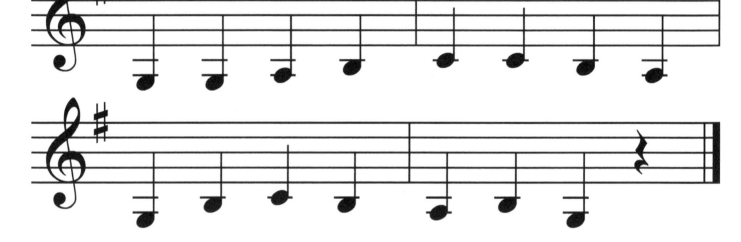

Second Tune on the G String with G, A, B and C
Zweites G-Saiten-Liedchen mit den Tönen G, A, H und C

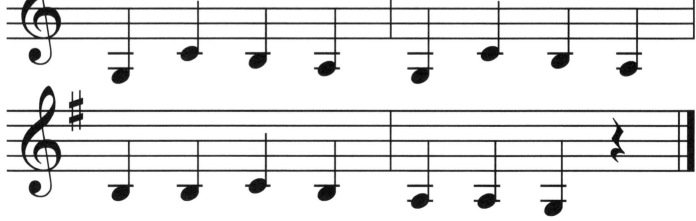

Piano Introduction for the Tunes 50 and 51 - Klaviervorspiel für die Liedchen 50 und 51

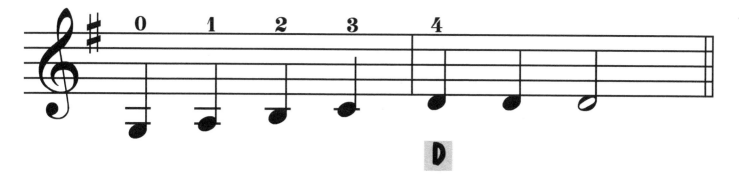

First Tune on the G String with G, A, B, C and D
Erstes G-Saiten-Liedchen mit den Tönen G, A, H, C und D

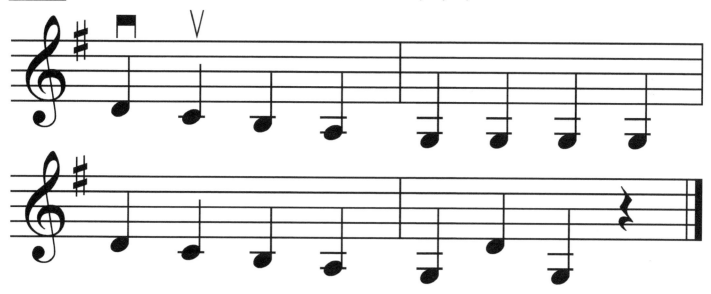

Second Tune on the G String with G, A, B, C and D
Zweites G-Saiten-Liedchen mit den Tönen G, A, H, C und D

52 Benny Hops on the G String · Benny springt auf der G-Saite

53 Benny Strolls on the G String · Benny bummelt auf der G-Saite

54 Benny Sleeps on the G String · Benny schläft auf der G-Saite

55 Benny Runs on the G String · Benny läuft auf der G-Saite

My First Compositions · Meine ersten eigenen Lieder

Composed by/Komponiert von _____ on/am _____

Begin and end your compositions with the indicated notes. You should choose and write all of the other notes. You might try plucking a few different melodies on your violin before writing your favorite for each string on the staves below.

Beginne und beende Deine Lieder mit den vorgegebenen Noten. Alle anderen Töne kannst Du selbst erfinden. Vielleicht zupfst Du erst einmal einige Melodien auf Deiner Geige, probierst sie aus und schreibst danach Deine Lieblingsmelodien von jeder Saite in die leeren Notenzeilen.

Melody on the D String · Lied auf der D-Saite

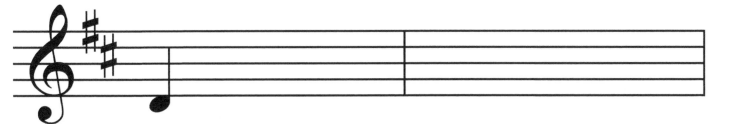

Melody on the G String · Lied auf der G-Saite

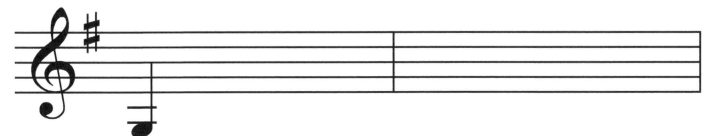

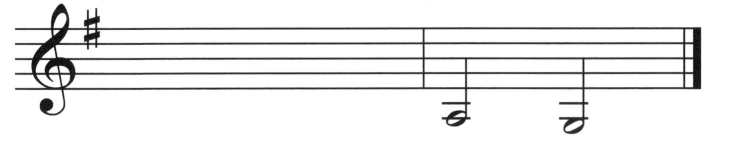

Final Test * Abschlußtest

What are the names of these notes? Enter the note names in the boxes below and the finger numbers above each note.

Wie heißen diese Noten? Schreibe die Notennamen auf die untere Zeile und die Fingerzahl über die Note.

1. G String • G-Saite

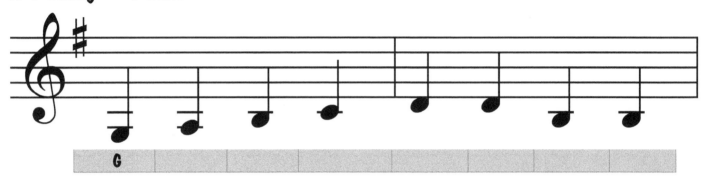

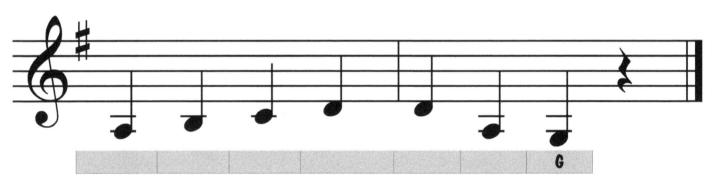

2. D String • D-Saite

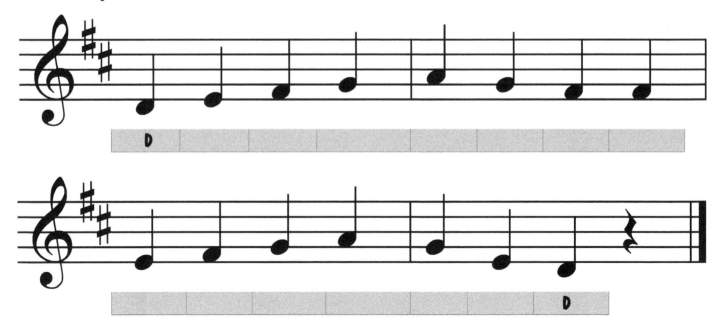

3. A String · A-Saite

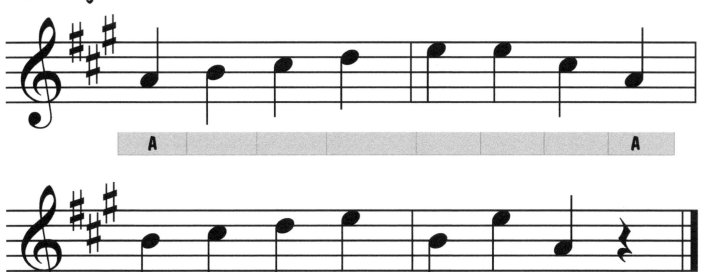

4. E String · E-Saite

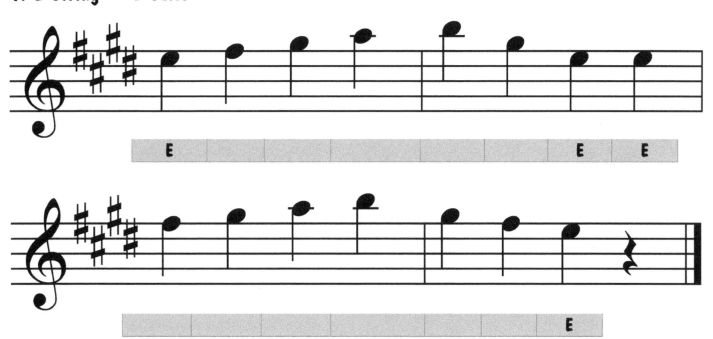

Congratulations!

You have now completed the first note-reading book.

Many new challenges await you in the next book, including

♦ Accidentals (Playing in different finger patterns)
♦ Different meters
♦ New note values
♦ Dynamic and articulation markings

Herzlichen Glückwunsch!

Du bist am Ende des ersten Notenlesebuches angekommen.

Im nächsten Heft erwarten Dich viele neue Aufgaben u.a. mit folgenden Themen:

♦ Vorzeichen (Spielen in verschiedenen Griffstellungen)
♦ Verschiedene Taktarten
♦ Weitere Notenwerte
♦ Dynamische und Artikulationszeichen

Solutions to the Brain Teasers - Auflösung der Rätsel

Brain Teaser No. 1 - Ratespiel Nr. 1

| D | D | E | E | F#/Fis | A | D | D |

| E | E | A | G | F#/Fis | E | D |

Which number is this "Leaf Melody" in the book?
Welche Nummer hat das Blätter-Lied in diesem Heft?

14

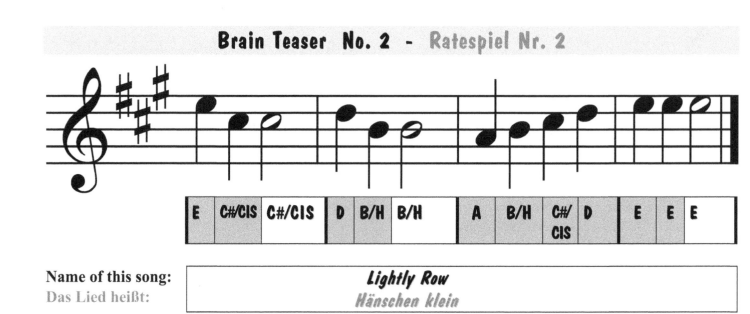

Brain Teaser No. 2 - Ratespiel Nr. 2

| E | C#/CIS | C#/CIS | D | B/H | B/H | A | B/H | C#/CIS | D | E | E | E |

Name of this song: *Lightly Row*
Das Lied heißt: *Hänschen klein*

46

Brain Teaser No. 3 - Ratespiel Nr. 3

Tune on the E string with 10 mistakes   Lied auf der E-Saite mit 10 Fehlern

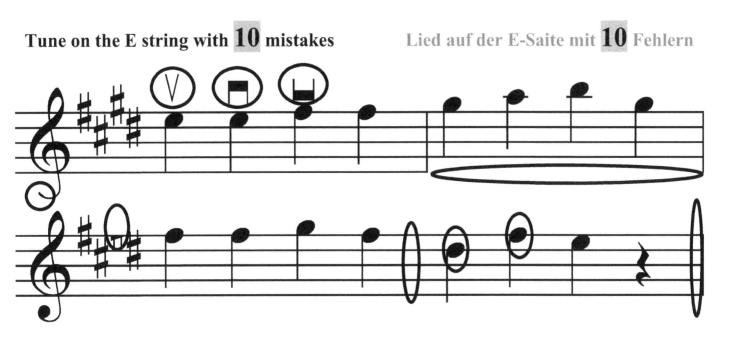

Solutions to the Final Test - Auflösung des Abschlusstests

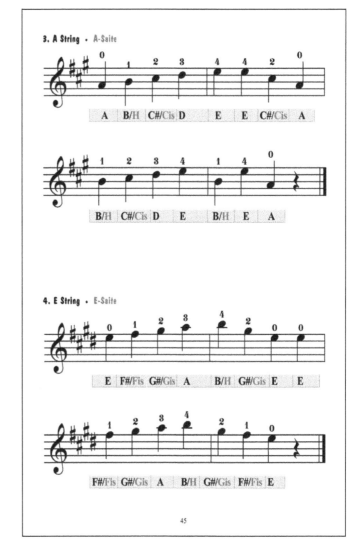